Double-Dip Feelings

Stories to Help Children Understand Emotions

SECOND EDITION

written by
Barbara Cain, M.S.W.

illustrated by
Anne Patterson

MAGINATION PRESS • WASHINGTON, DC

For Al, Steve, Gina, and Ken — BC

Published by
M A G I N A T I O N   P R E S S
An Educational Publishing Foundation Book
American Psychological Association
750 First Street, NE
Washington, DC 20002

For more information about our books, including a complete catalog, please write to us, call 1-800-374-2721, or visit our website at www.maginationpress.com.

Editor: Darcie Conner Johnston
Art Director: Susan K. White
The text type is Quorum.

Library of Congress Cataloging-in-Publication Data

Cain, Barbara S.
Double-dip feelings / written by Barbara S. Cain ;
illustrated by Anne Patterson. — Rev. ed.
p. cm.
ISBN 1-55798-812-9 (alk. paper) — ISBN 1-55798-811-0 (pbk. : alk. paper)
1. Ambivalence — Juvenile literature.
2. Emotions — Juvenile literature.
[1. Emotions.] I. Patterson, Anne, ill. II. Title.

BF575.A45 C35 2001
155.4'124 — dc21   2001030832

Manufactured in the United States of America
10 9 8 7 6 5 4 3 2 1

Everyone has feelings.

There are many different kinds.

AND

Sometimes we have TWO at the very same time.

Sometimes we feel happy.

Sometimes we feel sad.

AND

Sometimes we feel
BOTH happy and sad.

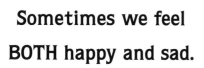

4

Sometimes we feel playful.

Sometimes we feel mad.

Sometimes we feel BOTH playful and mad.

Did you ever have two different feelings
at the very same time?

When Kevin began his first day of school,
he felt big boy PROUD

and little boy SCARED.

When Amy's new brother came home to live,
she felt somersault JOY

and left-out SAD.

When he painted her face with an oatmeal fist,

Amy said, "He's a funny little boy but a very big pest."

Did you ever feel both SILLY and MAD

at the very same time?

When Katie's family moved to a different town,
She said, "I like my new house with a room of my own."

"The old one was smaller but the old one was home."

Did you ever feel both HAPPY and SAD
at the very same time?

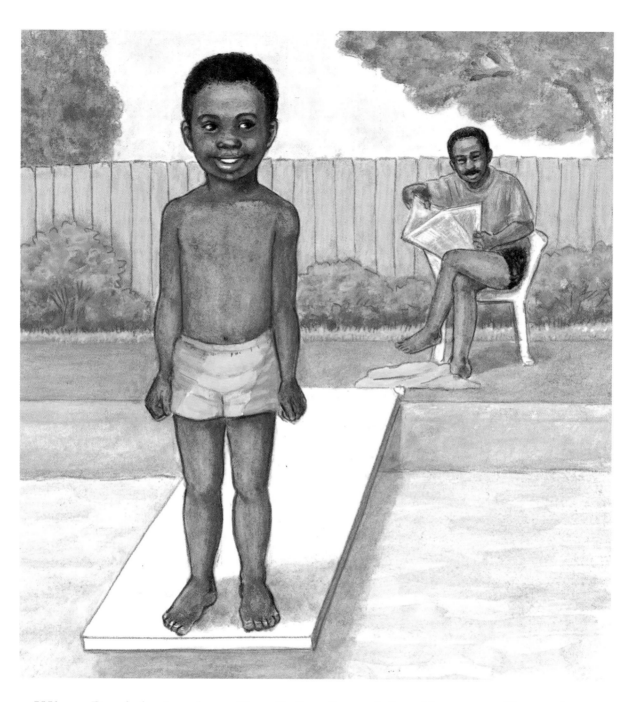

When Daniel stood on the diving board for the very first time,
He thought, "I promised my dad I would do it,
But I wish I could change my mind."

Did you ever feel both BRAVE and AFRAID

at the very same time?

When classmates teased Sam for wetting his pants,
Kevin thought, "I want to tease him too,
but he's only doing what I used to do."

Did you ever feel both MEAN and FRIENDLY
at the very same time?

When Daniel beat Amy in a spelling bee at school,

he was THRILLED to be a winner,

but WORRIED that he would lose a friend.

When Katie had chicken pox in bright shades of red,
she HATED all the itchy spots,

but LOVED being cozy
with Gigi in bed.

When Katie dumped her dinner in Gigi's plate,
she was GLAD to be rid of her spinach,

but SORRY she gave him a snack he would hate!

When Kevin was leaving for an overnight sleep,
he said, "I know I'll look silly when I bring my bear,
but he can't sleep when I'm not there."

Did you ever feel both EMBARRASSED and EXCITED
at the very same time?

When darkness fell and it was time for bed,
Amy ENVIED the kids playing hide and seek,

but she was GLAD

to go to sleep.

So, if sometimes you feel both happy AND sad,
and sometimes you feel both friendly AND mad,

Remember, everyone has feelings.

There are many different kinds.

And sometimes we have TWO at the very same time.

About Double-Dip Feelings

by Jane Annunziata, Psy.D.

A Note to Children

Now that you have read this book, you have started to learn about "double-dip" feelings. They are called "double-dip" because they are two different feelings that happen at the same time, sort of like two flavors of ice cream scoops right on top of each other. With an ice cream cone, double dips are fun, because you get to have twice as much ice cream as a single scoop. But with feelings, double dips usually aren't so much fun. When kids have these kinds of feelings, they often feel confused and uncomfortable. It bothers kids to feel two different ways at the same time because they don't quite know what to do. Here are some ideas to help you with your double-dip feelings:

 It helps to know that double-dip feelings are very common, normal, and OK! Everyone has them sometimes, even grown-ups. It's just part of having feelings. Some are single and some are double.

When you are trying to decide what to do when you feel two opposite ways, think about which feeling will make you feel good about yourself. Like on page 16 when kids are teasing Sam for wetting his pants, Kevin could "solve" his double-dip feelings by saying, "Well, I feel mean and friendly at the very same time. But I am going to feel really bad about myself if I act mean. If I act friendly, I'll feel really good about myself. Plus, Sam will feel better too. I think I know what to do with my double-dip feelings now. I'll act friendly."

Sometime double-dip feelings feel better, and kind of get solved too, if we just say out loud what we are feeling. It makes things a lot less confusing. Let's say you are feeling thrilled and worried when you win a contest, like Daniel on pages 18 and 19. Daniel was worried that he would lose Amy as a friend. That probably made it hard for him to enjoy his thrilled feelings. But if he could just talk with Amy about his worry, he would probably find that she will still be his friend, even though she might be a little sad about losing. This idea of just talking about our feelings to help them feel better sounds so simple, but it really works.

The last thing to remember about double-dip feelings is that the ones that worry you or scare you usually get easier as you get older and as you get more used to new things. For instance, the scared feelings that kids have when they start a new school (like Kevin on pages 6 and 7) usually get smaller as the day goes on and the proud feelings get bigger. Just knowing this ahead of time can help the scary feelings seem not so scary, even at the beginning.

Now that you have some ideas about what to do with your double-dip feelings, you probably won't be so bothered by them. You will have lots of chances to practice these ideas and to feel OK with these feelings, because there are so many of them around! You can do it!

A Note to Parents

DOUBLE-DIP FEELINGS is a book about ambivalence, the experience of having different and opposing feelings at the same time. As a child reads the various situations in the book—many of which are familiar to all children, such as starting school or getting a new baby brother or sister—he or she learns to label the ambivalent feelings that typically occur. The child learns, thus, that two opposite feelings can happen in concert, and that this phenomenon is actually rather common. These are important lessons for the developing emotional self.

Ambivalence is discomforting even to adults, who have the ability to understand and tolerate opposing feelings. For children, ambivalent feelings are far more uncomfortable and confusing, because children's intellectual and emotional resources for tolerating them are more limited and less developed. As parents, you may be able to draw from your own grow-up difficulties to imagine just how hard it is for your inexperienced child to accept and resolve ambivalent feelings.

Parents can help their children both tolerate conflicting feelings and resolve them in a number of concrete ways:

Encourage children in the direction that will preserve or enhance good feelings about themselves. For example, when reading page 16, on which Sam has wet his pants and Kevin feels both friendly and mean at the same time, you might ask your child, "What would make you feel better about yourself? If you acted mean or if you acted friendly?" Or you could say, "I'm not sure you would like yourself very much if you made fun of your friend for wetting his pants." Indeed, parents can use a vignette like this as an opportunity to build empathy in their child by saying, "How do you think Sam feels when he is teased for wetting his pants?" This question can lead to, "Maybe realizing how bad Sam feels when he is teased can help you decide how you want to act—that is, that you'd rather act friendly." In this process, the ambivalence is resolved.

Help your child express feelings constructively rather than just holding on to the uncomfortable ambivalence. For example, Daniel is both worried and thrilled about winning the spelling bee (pages 18-19), and Amy is both joyous and sad about her new baby brother (pages 8-9). Parents can use these vignettes and others as jumping-off points to discuss the benefits of expressing a concern. Thus, you and your child might decide that Daniel could say to his friend, "I am worried that you won't be my friend because I beat you in the spelling bee," or that Amy could say to her mom and dad, "I'm worried that there won't be room for me since the new baby came, but I'm happy about it too." These statements are springboards to conversations that can open lines of communication and move the child beyond his or her disturbing confusion, thereby resolving the ambivalence.

Encourage your child in the direction of growth and movement up his or her developmental ladder by fostering optimism. For example, Kevin is scared about the first day of school (pages 6-7), and Daniel is frightened by the diving board (pages 14-15). In such situations, children can be assisted with positive messages such as, "You might feel scared at the beginning of the day, but as the day goes on it will get easier and easier (and it will!), and you will feel so proud," and "The thought of jumping off the diving board is scary, but usually doing it is much easier than thinking about it."

JANE ANNUNZIATA, PSY.D., is a clinical psychologist with a private practice for children and families in McLean, Virginia. She is also the author of several books addressing concerns of children and parents.